CHANGES

7 BIBLICAL LESSONS TO MAKE SENSE OF PUBERTY

LUKE AND TRISHA GILKERSON

INTOXICATEDONLIFE.COM

STOP! Before You Get Started...

WATCH THESE 3 *FREE* VIDEOS

Thank you for purchasing our book! Take a moment to check out 3 free videos we've put together on talking to kids about sex. We'll teach you...

- The 2 essential Biblical truths about sex you must pass on to your kids
- 3 parenting style you want to be sure to avoid
- Why it's important to begin talking about sex sooner than you think

IntoxicatedOnLife.com/TalkVideos

Changes: 7 Biblical Lessons to Make Sense of Puberty

All contents copyright 2015 by Luke and Trisha Gilkerson. All rights reserved.

No part of this document may be reproduced or transmitted in any form, by any means (electronic, photocopying, recording, or otherwise) without the prior written permission of the publisher.

If you have this file and have not paid for it, please be sure to visit
IntoxicatedOnLife.com to pay for your own copy.
The author of this book put many hours into working on this Bible study.

This publication is protected under the US Copyright Act of 1976 and all other applicable international, federal, state, and local laws, and all rights are reserved.

Publishing and Design Services by MelindaMartin.me

CONTENTS

Introduction for Parents 1

Just Like Jesus: Growing in Wisdom and Stature 10

Puberty: Just One of Many Changes 13

Hormones: The Catalyst of Change 16

Girls and Boys: Changes We Can Both Expect 22

Girl Changes: Becoming a Woman 27

Boy Changes: Becoming a Man 33

Changes in Desire: The Goodness of Sexual Attraction 39

What's Next? 43

Having the Talk

Do you feel overwhelmed, confused, or uncertain on how to introduce your young children to Biblical sexuality?

Having the Talk is a video series for Christian parents, including 8 video lessons and 3 mini bonus lessons. Luke and Trisha Gilkerson walk through each of the concepts presented in their book, *The Talk: 7 Lessons to Introduce Your Child to Biblical Sexuality* (for kids 6-10), and explain how to talk about each concept.

In addition, Luke and Trisha answer many frequently asked questions, including topics some parents find really uncomfortable, such as

- what you say if your child thinks the whole concept of sex is gross
- what to do if you find out your child has been looking at sexually inappropriate media
- what to do if you catch your child masturbating
- what to say when your child tells you they have been thinking about sex
- when your child asks about sensitive topics like abortion or children born out of wedlock or homosexuality or transgenderism

Check out the series of videos at IntoxicatedOnLife.com/having-the-talk.

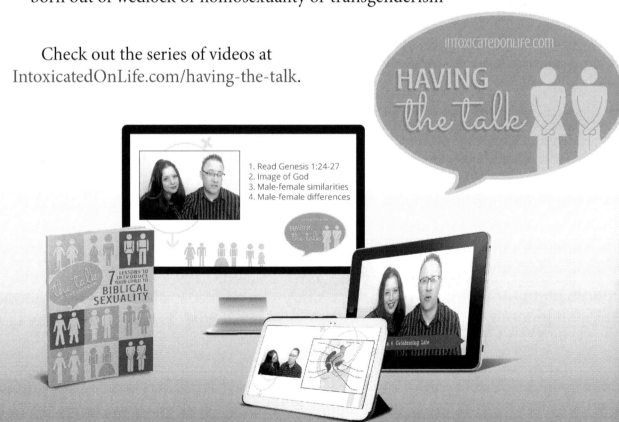

the talk: biblical sex education series

Changes: 7 Biblical Lessons to Make Sense of Puberty
is the second in a series of devotional books for families focusing on sex education.

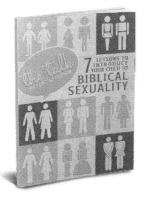

The Talk: 7 Lessons to Introduce Your Child to Biblical Sexuality
This book is for kids ages 6-10 and introduces basic concepts, such as the differences between male and female anatomy, how babies are conceived and grow in the womb, and the importance of saving sex until marriage.

Changes: 7 Biblical Lessons to Make Sense of Puberty – This book is geared towards kids ages 8-12 and introduces children to the physical and emotional changes that puberty brings.

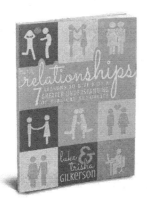

Relationships: 7 Lessons to Give Kids a Greater Understanding of Biblical Sexuality – Designed for parents to use with their children ages 11+, *Relationships* gives parents talking points about how to steward one's own sexuality. Topics include information about gender, lust, masturbation, pornography, modesty, homosexuality, and guarding the heart. Go to IntoxicatedOnLife.com/relationships to learn how you can be notified when it is released in Spring 2016.

Learn more about the whole series at
IntoxicatedOnLife.com/store.

INTRODUCTION FOR PARENTS

What This Study Is and How to Use It

This is a series of seven devotional Bible studies to read with your child, providing a foundational understanding of the changes that happen during puberty. It looks at puberty from God's perspective.

This book is designed specifically for children ages 8 to 12, discussed over seven days.

Why a Sex Ed Family Devotional?

Not too long ago we wrote our first book in this series, <u>The Talk: 7 Lessons to Introduce Your Child to Biblical Sexuality</u>, a book especially for kids 6 to 10 years old. The book was more or less a natural outcropping of a couple significant situations in our life.

First and foremost, our oldest son was gradually growing more curious about sexual topics. Our conversations with him on sexual matters had always been fairly natural, brief, and laid-back, but we knew the time was right to have some more formal conversations with him and lay some biblical groundwork about the purpose of sex.

We did our homework and found many great resources teaching parents about sex education—even some great resources from a Christian perspective—but we never found the book we were really looking for. We wanted his sex education to be a natural extension of the family devotions and the home education we were already doing. We were already in the habit of sitting with him and his brothers most evenings, opening the Scriptures with them, and talking about how the Bible applies to our lives. We wanted him to learn about sex the same way, focusing on God's Word (with a healthy dose of biology thrown in for good measure).

In many ways, *The Talk* was a desire to create the book we never found.

The second significant situation that served as a catalyst for the book was Luke's job at <u>Covenant Eyes</u>. For years my job has been to educate families and individuals about the dangers

INTRODUCTION FOR PARENTS

that can be found online—especially pornography. In that time, I've spoken with *a lot* of parents who wish they would have taken the time to really talk to their kids about sex before the Internet or friends did. I've spoken to many men and women who grew up in deeply religious homes where sex was a taboo subject—even a dirty subject—which served as one of the key ingredients in their beginning obsession with pornography, fantasy, and promiscuity. Every week, I hear traumatic and heartbreaking stories.

As parents, we more or less take it for granted that our kids will see pornography someday. We know they will be exposed to sexual media and sexually perverse conversations. But as far as we are able, we want to be the first and dominant voice our kids hear when it comes to the subject of sex.

Just Give Me a Script

After publishing *The Talk*, we were overwhelmed with the response from parents. Of course, we had our fair share of nay-sayers—parents who thought it was appalling someone would talk to their child about sex so young. But the dominant response we heard was: "Thank you. This takes the edge off my own nervousness and gives me a script to follow."

Since that time we have learned, for many families, the biggest barriers to sex education are parental negligence and parental nervousness. You may be the negligent type, procrastinating on important conversations—but maybe not anymore since you've decided to read this book. You might also be the nervous type. You understand, deep down, sex is an important topic, and you can't bring yourself just to "wing it" when it comes to broaching the subject with your kids. We completely get that.

Let this book and its prequel, *The Talk*, help you break the ice. Read them aloud word for word. Or read them aloud and interject your own thoughts. Or just read them ahead of time to give you a basic outline for what you want to say. Do what feels most natural for you and your children.

As we are able, we want to be the first and dominant voice our kids hear when it comes to the subject of sex.

Foundational Building Blocks of Biblical Sexual Values

The series of lessons in this book covers basic theological and biological concepts about puberty in a language children can understand. Each study is anchored in a specific text of Scripture.

- **Lesson 1** looks at the adolescent years of Jesus, talking about how the culture in which Jesus lived recognized puberty as an important phase of physical and spiritual development. The goal of this lesson is to help your child see these changes not as something bizarre, but as something good. Even the Son of God Himself went through them.

- **Lesson 2** looks at the process of change in the human body throughout all of life. Puberty is just one of several significant phases men and women go through as they age. Physical changes are a normal part of life and nothing to fear.

- **Lesson 3** addresses the mental and emotional changes of puberty, as well as the internal catalyst for change in our bodies: hormones. The goal of this lesson is to teach children there are natural internal mechanisms in the body that guide the process of puberty—created by a loving, wise, and sovereign God.

- **Lesson 4** looks at the overall physical changes common to both boys and girls, including basic changes like height, body hair, body odor, acne, etc. This is all part of the natural transition to adulthood.

- **Lesson 5** deals with the changes that take place in girls during puberty, such as fat deposits, breast development, and menstruation. These changes are a natural part of what it means to be female.

- **Lesson 6** is about changes that take place in boys during puberty, such as muscular growth, facial hair, voice changes, testicular growth, and ejaculation. These changes are a natural part of what it means to be male.

- **Lesson 7** will delve into physical attraction. The Bible describes physical attraction as both very good and very powerful. Our kids need to understand both its goodness and power if they are going to steward their sexual development well during puberty.

The Bible and Puberty

The Bible says very little about puberty because it was more or less an assumed fact of life for biblical authors.

INTRODUCTION FOR PARENTS

The Jewish teachers in Jesus' day, and in the centuries following, considered ages 12 and 13 to be the age of accountability and the age of physical maturity—this was when puberty was in full bloom and when adulthood began. After this transition, the young boy or girl was responsible to take upon himself or herself God's commandments and religious duties.

A year prior to this official transition to adulthood, Jewish boys and girls were brought to the temple in Jerusalem for one of the religious feasts for a special blessing from the rabbis. This is most certainly the cultural background of the story of Jesus at the temple at 12 years old (Luke 2:42). Jesus' parents and community could see Jesus was becoming an adult man, and they marked that occasion by a very special visit to the temple to worship God.

Both the person of Jesus and the example of Jesus' culture should be instructive for us as Christian parents. First, the transition to physically and sexually mature adulthood should be seen as a good thing—not something to speak about in hushed tones but something that marks a purposeful and significant transition in life. Second, when God the Son was born in the likeness of man, He did not think himself above the process of puberty. He experienced the same hormones and physical changes we all do. This only further dignifies puberty, not merely as a clumsy phase of emerging zits and embarrassing body odor, but as good change enacted by a good God.

How Soon is Too Soon? (And Why Are You Asking?)

Most parents know the ripe old age of 2 is probably too soon to talk about puberty, and 25 is probably too late. Beyond this, a lot of parents are lost.

We've written this study for kids ages 8 to 12, but that's a pretty broad range. When is this study right for *your* child?

First, let's address not the question itself but the possible reasons behind the question. If the question is motivated by a desire for your child to be able to comprehend these ideas because of his or her intellectual development or attention span, then you're asking a very relevant question. There's no sense in dumping information into your child when it will easily be forgotten or misapplied. There's a reason we don't teach calculus to 3-year-olds.

If, however, the question is motivated by a desire to postpone the conversation because you don't want to rob a child of his or her "innocence," then it might be good to challenge your assumptions. Focus on the Family's *The Complete Book of Baby & Child Care*, wisely says,

> "Giving a child facts about reproduction, including details about intercourse, does not rob him of innocence. Innocence is a function of attitude, not information. A school-

age child who understands the specifics of sex, while seeing it as an act that, in the proper context, both expresses love and begins new life, retains his innocence. But a child who knows very little about sex can already have a corrupt mind-set if he has been exposed to it in a degrading, mocking, or abusive context."

As parents, we need to challenge the unbiblical belief that merely knowing information about sex robs a child of something—other than ignorance. It simply doesn't.

What does rob a child of innocence is exposure to the *abuse* of sex. We live in an age where this problem is rampant, which means parents not only need to do all in their power to guard and protect young eyes and ears from sexually exploitative material, they also need to establish themselves as the sexual authorities in the home earlier than in previous generations. When a 6-year-old comes home wondering what a "blow job" is because she heard about it on the playground, or when a 9-year-old is shocked by the images he just saw appear on the screen during a Google search, these kids need to know their parents are available and very willing to level with them in honest conversations without fear or shame.

In other words, if by supplying you with an age range for this book, your tendency is to postpone teaching it to the absolute latest age, understand that is not the intention. God invented puberty for one fairly obvious reason: it is His natural process for transforming your children into adults capable of sexual reproduction at some point in the future. Our children are sexual beings—gendered from birth and set on a trajectory toward mature manhood or womanhood. That may be a hard pill for you to swallow, but it may be high time to choke it down.

So when is the best time to talk about puberty specifically? The short answer is this: *it is a good time to talk about puberty when your child can make good use of the information.* For many kids, this means talking about puberty some time right before or right as overt signs of puberty are first visible in their own bodies, or—and this is important—when signs of it are visible in the lives of their peers. Delaying the conversation because *your* child is a late bloomer is unwise because others around them are experiencing obvious changes he or she needs to understand.

Dr. James Tanner, a pediatric endocrinologist, identified five stages of puberty—now called the Tanner Stages. These stages of sexual maturity are marked by penis and testes growth in boys, breast development in girls, and pubic hair growth in both genders.

 Kids need to know their parents are available and very willing to level with them in honest conversations without fear or shame.

INTRODUCTION FOR PARENTS

Stage	Female					Male				
	Age Range	Breast Growth	Pubic Hair Growth	Other Changes	Age Range	Testes Growth	Penis Growth	Pubic Hair Growth	Other Changes
I	0-15	Pre-adolescent	None	Pre-adolescent	0-15	Pre-adolescent testes	Pre-adolescent	None	Pre-adolescent
II	8-15	Breast buds appear and the areola begins to grow	Long downy pubic hair near the labia, often appearing with breast budding or several weeks or months later	Peak growth velocity often occurs soon after stage II	10-15	Enlargement of testes; pigmentation of scrotal sac	Minimal or no enlargement	Long downy hair, often appearing several months after testicular growth;	Not applicable
III	10-15	Further enlargement of breast tissue and areola, with no separation of their contours	Increase in amount and pigmentation of hair	First menstrual cycle occurs in 2% of girls late in stage III	11.5-16.5	Further enlargement	Significant enlargement, especially in diameter	Increase in amount; curling	Not applicable
IV	10-17	Separation of contours; areola and nipple form secondary mound above breasts tissue	Adult in type but not in distribution	First menstrual cycle occurs in most girls in stage IV, 1-3 years after breast budding	Variable: 12-17	Further enlargement	Further enlargement, especially in diameter	Adult in type but not in distribution	Development of axillary hair and some facial hair
V	12.5-18	Large breast with single contour	Adult in distribution	First menstrual cycle occurs in 10% of girls in stage V.	13-18	Adult in size	Adult in size	Adult in distribution	Body hair continues to grow and muscles continue to increase in size for several months to years; 20% of boys reach peak growth velocity during this period

Puberty officially begins at Stage II. For girls, on average, the development of breast buds is between the age of 8 to 10, though for some girls it is still biologically normal to see this as young as 7 or even 6 (depending on your family background). This is usually followed weeks or months later by pubic hair growth near the labia. For boys, between the ages of 9 and 11 (but sometimes as late as 15), the testes begin to grow and the skin on the scrotum begins to thin and redden. This is also usually followed by initial pubic hair growth. (Of course, if you have questions about the timing of sexual development in your children, consult your family physician or pediatrician.)

For these reasons, depending on how your child's own body is developing and depending on the physical development of those your child is around, it could be perfectly fitting to go through this material around 8 years old, and for many kids, ages 9 or 10 would be ideal. By age 12, most children and their peers have moved beyond Stage II, and the conversation is probably somewhat overdue.

Also, it is important not to postpone these discussions based on what you remember from *your* own pubescent development. Many scientists now recognize children are beginning puberty younger with each generation. Many factors have been blamed for this, from environmental toxins to antibiotics in food to childhood obesity. Aside from these unforeseen considerations is the fact that every child is different: just because you were a late bloomer doesn't mean your child will be—and it certainly doesn't mean your child's friends will be.

Getting Over Your Fear of Sex

Puberty is a sexual topic and this frightens some parents. Some honestly believe there's something inherently naughty about sex. Some know sex is a good thing, but it is simply too embarrassing and personal. In a word, for some, sex is *gross*, a necessary function to continue the human race, but they'd rather not talk about it.

The rest of the world, however, treats sex as a *god*, an ultimate source of pleasure, meaning, and value.

Neither of these is a right biblical attitude. Sex is not *gross*; it is not *God*. But it is *good*. As parents, it is not only our job to communicate to our children what sex is, but a godly *attitude* about it. Our words and tone of voice should communicate to our children that sex is very *good*, created by God as a blessing.

As parents, we need to own up to the fact that our discomfort in talking about sex is simply that: *our* discomfort. Of course, shucking our discomfort doesn't mean trading prudish embarrassment for crass conversation—like meat-headed boys in the locker room. But it does

INTRODUCTION FOR PARENTS

mean getting comfortable with being frank and straightforward about sex so we can become our children's trusted source of information.

What should frighten us far more than the awkward thought of saying words like "penis" and "vagina" in the same sentence are the perverse things spoken by the world that will fill the void made by our silence.

Should You Talk About Both Boy and Girl Changes?

Some parents might be tempted to talk to their child about only the change their child's gender faces during puberty, but we would caution against that.

The changes that take place in both boys and girls are purposeful. There is a divine design to these changes. Boys need to know about the changes that take place in girls, and girls need to know about the changes that take place in boys. This knowledge not only somewhat de-mystifies the opposite sex, it also introduces your child to all the wonders of the human body and the way God uniquely suited men and women. Not to mention, it is quite difficult to talk to kids about what a sperm is for or what an egg is for without mentioning the other.

Is Your Child Ready for *This* Study?

Think of the information in this study as *seeds* you are sowing into your child. In what kinds of *soil* do these seeds grow best?

The Soil of Familiarity

There's a fair amount of biological information in these lessons. Ideally, children should grow up in a home very comfortable with conversations about how our bodies work. From early childhood, parents should model a balance of talking frankly about the body and a sense of modesty and propriety. For example, a child should know correct names for body parts and be taught to show respect for privacy.

If your child has not learned the kind of material we teach in our first book, <u>The Talk</u>, consider that book as a stepping stone to this one. That book covers material such as the basic biological differences between male and female (inside and outside), how babies are made, what intercourse is, what adultery is, and why sex is only for married couples. These basic conversations about human sexuality allow the conversations about puberty to make much more sense. Without them, there is no context for making sense of puberty.

The Soil of Formative Teaching

This study assumes you are in a habit of sitting down regularly with your child to read the Bible, pray, and discuss what specific ideas mean. These lessons should ideally feel like *normal* and *natural* extensions of your family devotions. If this isn't part of the rhythm of your home yet, don't start with this study. Start by establishing a regular routine of conversation about the Bible coupled with prayer. Get comfortable as a spiritual leader in your home. After you have several months of this under your belt, then consider using this study.

The Soil of Familial Love

Sexual education isn't just taught. It is modeled. Married parents should model what romantic love looks like—honoring and cherishing one another, stealing kisses in the hallway, dancing in the living room, compliments, gifts, etc. Single parents should honor God's standards of celibacy and sexual integrity in their dating relationships. Parents need to model virtues of modesty and honoring the dignity of others—in how we speak about others, in our media choices, and in how we interact. The value and centrality of this modeling cannot be overstated.

The First of Many Conversations

If there ever was a time when parents could have a single sex talk and be done with conversations about sexuality for good, those days are long gone. Teaching children about sex is not a one-time thing. Parents are to teach their children the commands of God repeatedly and in the day-to-day situations of life, "when you sit in your house, and when you walk by the way, and when you lie down, and when you rise" (Deuteronomy 6:7).

Along with <u>The Talk</u>, these lessons can provide your child with foundational teachings, but after the foundation is laid, more is needed. Repetition is the mother of learning. As time goes on, you'll need to reinforce these lessons in the moment-by-moment situations of life. As your child gets older, you'll want to give more knowledge as it pertains to their growing sexual interests.

Puberty is Good

Christians, of all people, should embrace puberty with excitement. Like many of life's transitions, this one may have its awkward moments, but they are moments filled with purpose. Teach your children to see these changes through the eyes of a sovereign God, their wise Creator. We pray these lessons give you the language to do just that.

JUST LIKE JESUS: GROWING IN WISDOM AND STATURE

Opening Thought:

The Bible says something amazing about Jesus: He is both God and human at the same time. This means before time began, He lived with God the Father and had all the same characteristics of God. He is all-powerful, present everywhere, all-knowing, unchanging, infinite, and not dependent on anything or anyone. But one day, He came to Earth as a human being. This means He set aside His glory and took up all the characteristics of being human.

So, even though Jesus is God, do you think He ever felt physical pain? (*Yes.*) Got tired? (*Yes.*) Got hungry? (*Yes.*) Got thirsty? (*Yes.*) Do you think Jesus had human emotions? (*Yes.*) He experienced all these things but without doing anything sinful that would displease His heavenly Father.

Jesus also grew up just like other children do. Let's read a story about that.

Scripture Reading: Luke 2:41-52

Explanation: This story is all about Jesus growing up. Something special happened when Jesus was 12 years old. Do you remember where Jesus was going with his parents? (The temple in Jerusalem.) They made the long trek with their family and friends from Nazareth, where Jesus grew up, to Jerusalem, which was an 80-mile walk. It probably took three or four days to walk that far. They did this because Jesus' family wanted to go to the temple to worship God for the special celebrations and ceremonies in Jerusalem.

Why do you think the author tells us Jesus is 12 years old? Is that an important detail? (*See what your child thinks of this.*) It *is* an important fact. You see, back then, the years leading up to your 12th and 13th birthdays were special years for a young boy or girl. Before this time, you were seen as just a child. But by age 13, you started to be treated more like an adult. In Jesus' day, by age 13, you started to work more alongside other adults, learning the trade of your family. You would be expected to go to all the religious celebrations and ceremonies and keep God's commandments like you were an adult. Some would even get married when they were 13. Can you imagine that?

But those ages were special years because they were a special transition time. The reason this was a special transition time is because Jesus' people knew our bodies start going through a lot of changes during that time—changes that will continue into the teenage years. A lot of those changes are things you can't see—happening on the inside. Some of those changes are on the outside of your body. God has made our bodies to go through stages of growth, and one of those stages is called puberty. Have you heard the word "puberty" before? (*See what your child already knows.*)

Talking Points:

- Your body has different sexual organs—parts that make a man a man or parts that make a woman a woman. Can you think of an example? (*See if your child can name a sexual organ in their body, external organs such as a penis or vagina, or internal organs like testicles or ovaries.*)

- Puberty is a time of sexual development. This means before puberty, your body isn't capable of reproduction—it's not able to create babies. But after puberty, your body is mature enough to reproduce. This doesn't mean you *should* try to have babies right away, but your body is getting ready for the possibility of your getting married and having a family of your own some day. Your body is growing into an adult body.

- Some of these changes might seem a little strange, but we should remember these changes are how God designed us. In fact, Jesus went through all these changes, too. The story we just read says that Jesus grew in wisdom and stature, meaning his body got bigger and more mature, and his mind also grew in understanding. He transitioned from being a child to being an adult, and going through puberty is an important phase along the way.

- This is why we don't have to be scared of these changes or confused about them. God is the one who made our bodies. Even God's own Son went through them—which means they are a normal part of being human. It's good to grow up and become an adult.

Questions for Your Child:

1. Have you noticed any changes in your own body or in the bodies of your friends that are your age or older? *(See if you child has noticed anything, such as in friends or siblings.)*

2. What does it mean when the Bible says Jesus grew in stature? *(It means he grew in size. His body got bigger and more mature.)*

3. What do you think it means when the Bible says Jesus grew in wisdom? *(He learned and got smarter. Around the ages of 11 and 12, your body doesn't just mature but your mind does as well. It is a great time in life to do exactly what Jesus did—grow in knowledge and develop an even deeper relationship with your Heavenly Father.)*

4. As we learn more about puberty, keep in mind that Jesus, the Son of God, went through similar changes in his own body, so these changes aren't weird. They are exactly how God designed you. Are you interested in learning more about it? *(See if your child has any questions about puberty. Let your child know you'll be unpacking a lot of information in the coming lessons.)*

Prayer: God, when we are children, we speak like children, think like children, and reason like children, but when we become men and women, we give up our childish ways (1 Corinthians 13:11). Help us, as we grow in stature, to also grow in wisdom, to grow in favor with You and with others, just as Your Son did (Luke 2:52). Jesus, You were tempted in all ways just as we are, but without sin, so we draw near to you now to ask You for mercy as we learn about this important topic (Hebrews 4:15-16). Amen.

CHANGES

PUBERTY: JUST ONE OF MANY CHANGES

Opening Thought:

This study is all about changes in your body. Puberty is one big stage of change. Do you remember what puberty is? (*See what your child remembers. Puberty is a time of sexual development, when your body becomes capable of creating and caring for children some day.*) There are all kinds of physical, mental, and emotional changes happening at a fast rate in your body during puberty.

But really, change isn't anything new. Changes have been happening in your body since the moment you were conceived and will continue to happen until the day you die. We are constantly changing. Change is a part of life.

Scripture Reading: Proverbs 20:29

Explanation: The Bible everywhere assumes that change is part of life. This proverb tells us young men are strong in mind and body, but old men are crowned with grey hair—which is a sign they have lived a long life and have experiences we can learn from. Young men may not always be wise, but they are often strong because of the changes their bodies have gone through, going from little children to being adults. Old men may not be strong, but they are often wise because of the changes they've experienced in their lives. Who do you know who has grey hair? (*See if your child can name someone you know.*)

Changes take place throughout our entire lives.

PUBERTY: JUST ONE OF MANY CHANGES

Talking Points:

- Change begins at conception. When the father's sperm fertilizes the mother's egg inside her, a new human being is formed. When these two special cells join together, that is the beginning of human life. What do you remember about sperm and eggs? (*See what your child remembers about where sperm are from and where eggs are from and how they come together.*)

- Change begins to happen rapidly after an egg is fertilized. The single-celled human being is called a zygote, and this divides into two cells only 24 hours after it is fertilized. Then those two cells divide into four cells. And those four cells divide into eight, and so on and so on. It takes just 10 weeks until all of the baby's important organs begin to function.

- It takes just nine months before that single-celled life becomes a full-term baby. Though a baby isn't considered fully developed until around 40 weeks, with the help of modern medicine, babies can live outside of their mothers' wombs much earlier than that.

- Infancy and toddlerhood is a time when there is a lot of physical growth. During this time, children will double their height and quadruple their weight. During this time, we become aware of our surroundings, and we learn that by talking, we can communicate with others. What are the biggest changes you've noticed in people you've known since they were a baby? (*See if your child can think of a younger child they've seen grow up—it could be a younger sibling or family member or friend. What major changes has your child noticed?*)

- During early childhood, we continue to grow and develop physically. We also become more social and learn how to interact with others. There's a lot of mental growth during this time as we're learning about our surroundings and developing our own interests.

- Puberty typically marks the beginning of what is called adolescence. The word "adolescence" simply means to grow up. It is the period of life where you develop from a child into an adult. Your body will physically change in many ways. You'll also begin to find that you think differently, feel differently, and relate to other people in different way than you did as a child.

- Over the next several lessons we're going to cover many of the changes that will be happening to you and to those of the opposite sex during puberty. We'll also answer some questions you might have about certain things happening to your body or things you might be feeling.

- After this, comes full adulthood. Changes continue to happen throughout adulthood up until a person dies. Our brains continue to develop. We might start families of our own and become moms and dads. As our bodies get even older, we start to experience certain weaknesses we never had before, and eventually everyone's body gets too old to keep going, and we die. Who is the oldest person you know? (*What characteristics do they notice about that older person's body that makes them look old?*)

We're going to begin our next lesson by talking about what actually *causes* the changes that take place in the body.

Questions for Your Child:

1. Some think the changes during puberty are really weird, but change is part of our entire lives. How much have you changed in your life so far? (*See how far back your child can remember. What is his or her first memory? Does your child remember being shorter? Skinnier? Liking more childish activities he or she doesn't like as much anymore?*)

2. I've gone thought a lot of changes, too. How old was I when you were born? (*Let your child do the math. Talk to your child about some of your memories of changes in your own body: early childhood, teenage years, young adulthood. Perhaps even pull out pictures of when you were their age. Share some of your favorite memories from that time in your life.*)

Prayer: God, thank You for creating our bodies. We are so wonderfully made (Psalm 139:14). As we get older, our outer self will waste away, but our inner self is being renewed day by day (2 Corinthians 4:16). No matter how old and frail our bodies get, thank You for making our hearts more like Your Son Jesus. No matter how young or old we are, help us to present our bodies to You as living sacrifices, worshiping and glorifying You with all we do (Romans 12:1-2; 1 Corinthians 10:31). Amen.

HORMONES: THE CATALYST OF CHANGE

Opening Thought:

Do you know what a catalyst is? A catalyst is something that causes a reaction. For instance, if I line up dominoes and I push the first one with my finger, what do you think is going to happen?

(*Show your child the dominoes picture or actually set up a big row of dominoes.*)

All of the dominoes fall. My finger, in this example, is the catalyst.

Hormones are the catalyst in your body that causes it to change and mature. Hormones are one of the big things responsible for causing your body to develop from a child's body into an adult's body.

Scripture Reading: Psalm 104:21-28

Explanation: This psalm mentions several great creatures, like lions that hunt on the land or large sea creatures that hunt in the oceans. If you study these animals, you learn how they get their food: they have to move around, looking for and killing their prey. They are skilled hunters. But this psalm says something interesting. This psalmist says these animals look to God for food and that God feeds them. So which is it? Do they have to *hunt* for their food or does God *give* them food? (*See how your child reacts to this.*)

The answer is *both*. God works through natural processes. God made the lion to hunt and the sea creatures to swim for their prey, so when these animals do as they were designed to do, God is feeding them. He works through the processes of nature He created.

The same is true in our own bodies. God has designed our body to go through changes during puberty, but He is still the one in control and guiding it all.

HORMONES: THE CATALYST OF CHANGE

Talking Points:

(Show your child the brain diagram, the male anatomy, and the female anatomy diagrams, using the talking points below.)

FEMALE ANATOMY

MALE ANATOMY

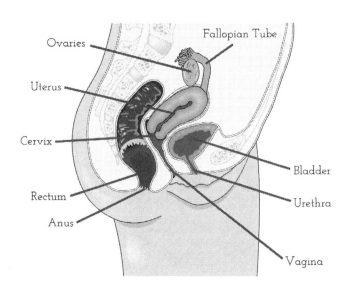

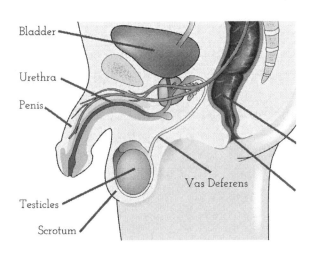

DIAGRAM OF A BRAIN

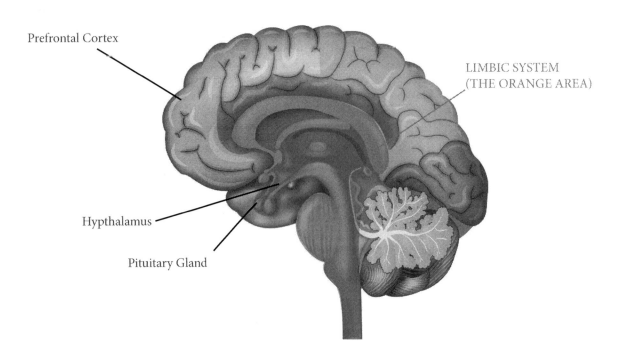

HORMONES: THE CATALYST OF CHANGE

Beginning in the Brain

- Remember the dominoes, how our finger is the catalyst? God has put something in our body called hormones that are catalysts. Hormones are very small chemical messengers. Different organs in your body produce these chemical messengers. They travel around your body and tell your body what it's supposed to do. During puberty, your body begins to produce hormones that are responsible for the changes happening in your body. Once these hormones start working, your body starts changing.

- We have a lot of different hormones in our body, but there are some very special hormones that our body begins to produce at puberty. There are two areas of our brain, the hypothalamus and pituitary gland: these are responsible for the start of puberty.

- Our hypothalamus produces something called GnRH (which is easier to say than gonadotropin-releasing hormone). GnRH tells the pituitary gland to release more hormones, and these hormones start the process of puberty.

- The pituitary gland is like the control center; it tells the other glands in your body what to do. When it sends out these special hormones, this signals the beginning of sexual development in both boys and girls. Look at how small the pituitary gland is—just the size of a pea. Isn't it amazing that this small gland control everything. *(Let your child see the diagram and see if they can hold up their fingers to show you how big a pea is.)*

The Physical Chain Reaction

- In girls, these hormones act on the ovaries. We'll talk about this in another lesson, but for now, just remember, the ovaries are responsible for releasing more hormones into the body like estrogen and progesterone. Estrogen is the primary hormone that is responsible for producing changes in a girl's body during puberty.

- Just like in girls, boys also begin puberty when the pituitary gland in the brain releases hormones. But in boys these hormones work on the testicles. We'll talk about this in another lesson, but for now just know that the testicles produce a hormone called testosterone. Testosterone is the primary hormone that is responsible for changes in a boy's body during puberty.

Mental and Emotional Changes

- As all these hormones start working in your body, there are a couple areas of your brain that go through some big changes during puberty— typically around age 11 for girls and a year later for boys. One of those areas is called the "limbic system." The limbic system has many important jobs, but one thing it does is drive our emotions. It's often called the "feeling brain."

- The second area of the brain that gets stronger during puberty is called the prefrontal cortex which is right behind your forehead. Let's call this your "thinking brain." This is the part of your brain that makes plans, thinks through options, and thinks about consequences. When emotions pop up in your feeling brain, it's your thinking brain that throws on the breaks and helps you to react in an appropriate way.

- But during puberty, your thinking brain is developing a little slower than your feeling brain. By your late teens, your thinking brain starts to catch up and it will continue to grow into your 20s. But in the meantime, there are probably going to be times when your emotions feel a little out of control: feelings of anger, fear, or excitement may come unexpectedly. You might feel like crying for no reason at all. Someone might say something that suddenly makes you feel really angry or sad. A lot of people called these "mood swings," because it looks like you are quickly swinging from one emotion to the next for no reason.

- When we feel really sad or mad, is that an excuse to sin against God or hurt someone else's feelings? (*No.*) Are these feelings a good reason to treat your friends or family poorly or to be disobedient? (*No.*) Puberty is a great time for you to practice what the Bible calls self-control. Self-control doesn't necessarily mean the ability to control your feelings. It means your ability to stop and think before you let your emotions control you. When you start to feel any strong emotions of sadness or anger, just remind yourself there's nothing wrong with those emotions, but ask God to help you not to let those emotions be your master. Hormones may influence us, but they shouldn't control us.

- As your feeling brain develops, you also might feel very brave and you want to take risks and try new things you've never done before. This is your feeling brain growing as you're learning how to think about actions and consequences. So, is puberty a great time to try new things and learn about your interests? Why? (*Yes. As you learn new skills, you learn about what you're really interested in and what you're good at, which prepares you for adult life.*)

- Of course, being risky can also backfire on you. Sometimes you might be tempted to do dangerous things, too. This is one of the reasons why God gives us parents—so as we grow and learn about the world, parents can help us make wise decisions.

- As your thinking brain develops, you'll be more able to think about things from other people's points of view, seeing issues and problems from different angles. This is a good thing, because it shows that your mind is growing. But the problem is you can also start to obsess

HORMONES: THE CATALYST OF CHANGE

over what other people might be thinking about *you*. You might start wondering, "Does that person like me? Do those people think I'm annoying? Do they think I'm cool? Do they want to be friends with me?" It is normal to have thoughts like this, but remember, what other people think of you doesn't matter nearly as much as what God thinks about you. The great news is if we are united with Christ, we have God's perfect favor and love.

Questions for Your Child:

1. So, do *hormones* cause us to go through puberty, or does *God* cause it to happen? *(Both. Just as God feeds the lions and sea creatures by working through their instinct to hunt for food, God also causes us to go through puberty by working through the natural release of these different hormones.)*

2. How are boys' and girls' bodies similar when it comes to puberty? *(We both have the same areas of the brain that release the same hormones. We both have reproductive organs that respond to these hormones. We both go through emotional changes as our brains grow and mature.)*

3. Thinking just about what we learned now, how are boys' and girls' bodies different? *(Boys have testicles which produce testosterone. Girls have ovaries that produce estrogen.)*

Prayer: God, just as You give food to the beasts and to the young ravens that cry out (Psalm 147:9), You created natural processes to make our bodies mature. You created human beings and delighted in Your creation, calling it very good (Genesis 1:31), and that includes our sexual maturity. You have called us to love you with all of our mind, so as our minds go through difficult emotions, give us self-control so our emotions don't become our master. The complexity and beauty of our bodies are a living witness to just how wise, powerful, and wonderful You are. Amen.

GIRLS AND BOYS: CHANGES WE CAN BOTH EXPECT

Opening Thought:

In the last lesson we talked about hormones. The hormones released in our bodies cause all the changes we go through during puberty. The first hormones that get released are ones in the brain. Do you remember the parts in a girl's body that release more hormones during puberty? (*Ovaries.*) Do you remember the parts in a boy's body that release hormones? (*Testicles.*)

Last time we talked about how your brain goes through big changes during puberty. What do you remember about some of the mental and emotional changes kids go through? (*Mood swings, desiring to try new things and be brave or take risks, being more self-conscious.*)

Did you know there are two times in our life when our brains go through the biggest growth spurt? The biggest time of change is when we are infants, but the second biggest time of change is during puberty.

The apostle Paul wrote some about the changes he went through during puberty in his first letter to the Corinthians.

Scripture Reading: 1 Corinthians 13:8-12

Explanation: Paul is thinking back on the time when he was becoming an adult, when he was going through puberty. Before this time, he was more childish in the way he thought, but as his brain and body grew, he could think and reason more like an adult.

Paul is making an analogy. He's trying to explain what it will be like after Jesus comes back to Earth. When Jesus comes back, the world will be perfect again and we will know Him fully—face to face. When we look back on our lives before Jesus came back, we will think, "We knew a lot about Jesus, but we really didn't know Him the way we do now. Before we got to see

Jesus face to face, we were like children in our understanding, but now that we can see Him, we really understand how amazing and awesome He is. It's like we have grown up." What do you think that will be like to see Jesus? (*Let your child imagine what it will be like to see Christ face to face.*)

Paul is using an experience all his readers can relate to. All his adult readers can understand what it was like to move from being a child to being an adult. They all remember the changes of puberty—both the mental changes and the physical changes. He's saying when we finally get to see Jesus and when He finally changes the world, it's like we will have become more mature. We will think differently, feel differently, and understand things differently.

For now, let's look at some of the big physical changes that both boys and girls go through during puberty.

Talking Points:

- Your body also goes through a lot of changes at this time. One big change is your height. Have you been getting taller all through your life? (*Yes.*) You have, but during puberty, you go through big growth spurts. This just means you get taller really quickly over a period of 2 or 3 years. Girls usually have a growth spurt between the ages of 10 and 14. Boys usually start their growth spurt a little later than girls, but they will often continue growing until their late teens, whereas girls stop growing much earlier.

- Also, keep in mind everyone goes through puberty at their own pace. Some start earlier. Some start later. Everyone's body looks different. This is why it is so important to never make fun of anyone because of the physical changes in their bodies. Their bodies were created by God, and God does not make mistakes.

- Another physical change is hair growth. At the beginning of puberty, you start growing hair around your genitals and in your armpits. The hair starts out soft, but eventually becomes thicker and sometimes darker and curlier. This is a sign your hormones are working properly and your sexual organs on the inside of your body are getting more mature. Do you know what this hair is called? (*See if your child knows. Tell him or her it is called pubic hair.*)

- Your body also sweats differently. You already sweat all over your body, but in places where you grow new hair, like your armpits or your genitals, you have what are called apocrine

GIRLS AND BOYS: CHANGES WE CAN BOTH EXPECT

glands. Before puberty, these glands aren't active, but they become active during puberty and will be for the rest of your life.

- These glands produce a special kind of sweat that is oilier. When this sweat gets to the surface of your body, bacteria on your skin really likes to eat it and these bacteria create a stinky smell when they eat. This is what causes body odor. Have you ever been next to a teenager or adult that had a really strong odor? *(See what your child says.)*

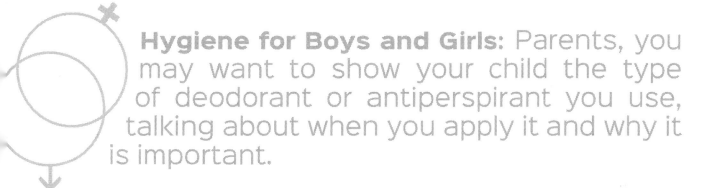

Hygiene for Boys and Girls: Parents, you may want to show your child the type of deodorant or antiperspirant you use, talking about when you apply it and why it is important.

- It's important when puberty starts to wash your body well if you don't want to smell bad.

- Also during puberty, some get what's called acne, which are swollen bumps on the skin, usually appearing on your face, neck, shoulders, or back.

- Your skin is covered in pores, which is where hair can grow. Nearly all of the skin on your body has pores, even though in a lot of places the hairs are very small and hard to see. These pores have glands that secrete an oily matter called sebum. Sebum is important because it keeps your skin and hair from drying out.

- But sometimes, especially during puberty, your body is creating a lot more sebum. Dead skin cells that are supposed to come out through your pores can then get trapped in the sebum, and the pores get clogged. Sometimes, the bacteria living on our skin can also get into these pores where they multiply and this can cause an infection. This is what acne is.

- Washing your skin both in the morning and at night is a good way to prevent acne. Eating a diet with plenty of whole foods like fruits, vegetables, protein, and healthy fats is also an important part of taking care of your skin. Too much sugar can cause acne to worsen. If doing these things isn't enough, we can look into other ways to help your have healthy skin.

- There might be times when you feel like you don't want these changes to happen, and it's normal to feel that way. Remember, it's a blessing to grow up and become an adult. Which of these changes sounds the most interesting to you? (*Get your child's opinion on which puberty changes sound the most interesting.*)

- You might feel uncomfortable with your physical changes at times, or you might feel like you don't like the look of your body. Just remember it is important not to compare yourself to how others look. Standards of what is pretty or handsome change all the time in our world, but God never changes. What He says about us is far more important than what other people think of us.

GIRLS AND BOYS: CHANGES WE CAN BOTH EXPECT

Questions for Your Child:

1. In some of your older friends or family, have you noticed any of these changes? *(Allow your child to think of someone slightly older. What changes are noticeable? Height? Body shape? Armpit hair? Mood swings? More desire for independence? Acne?)*

2. Which of these changes sound the strangest to you? *(Allow your child to express his or her discomfort about any of the things mentioned in this lesson. Be sure to reassure him or her that these changes are all part of the body's transition to adulthood.)*

3. A lot of the changes that happen in your body are in your private areas, and it's important we respect each other's privacy around our house. What are some things we can do around here to help each other have privacy when we're getting dressed or bathing? *(Locking doors, knocking before entering, asking for privacy when you need it, etc.)*

4. You've already gone through a lot of changes in your life, both in the way you think and in the way you look. Who is the one who made all those changes happen in your body? *(God. He is the one who created all the natural processes in our brain and body to create these changes.)*

Prayer: God, thank You for creating our bodies—we are fearfully and wonderfully made (Psalm 139:14). You are our Creator. It is You who made us, and we are Your people, the sheep of Your pasture (Psalm 100:3). As we get older, as we leave childhood behind, help us to put away childish things to become the kind of men and women You want us to be. We want to offer our bodies to You as living sacrifices, holy and pleasing to You, no matter what age of life we live (Romans 12:1). Amen.

CHANGES

GIRL CHANGES: BECOMING A WOMAN

Opening Thought:

What are some ways that boys and girls are very similar? (*Have your child answer this question. Point out the obvious similarities: both boys and girls have two eyes, a nose, a mouth, two ears, two legs, a heart, a brain, etc. Perhaps they will remember something from the previous lesson about how boys and girls both change during puberty.*).

What are some of the big differences you can see between boys and girls? (*See what your child notices. Your child might point out cultural differences, such as wearing different types of clothing, differences in common interests, or differences in body shape.*)

Almost every kind of creature in the world with a backbone has two sexes, male and female. This includes human beings. This is how God made us. Today, we're going to talk specifically about the changes that take place in girls during puberty.

Most girls begin puberty sometime between 8 and 15 years old, but there isn't any way of knowing for sure when your body will decide it's time to start. Puberty typically lasts anywhere from 2 to 5 years. Everyone's a little different, but what happens during puberty is pretty much the same for all girls.

Scripture Reading: Genesis 1:26-27

Explanation: God created both male and female. Men and women are similar in many ways. We are both created in the image of God, which means men and women deserve the same respect. We both have similar features. But there are some very important differences. God made men and women with different body parts, both inside and out. God also made men and women to develop differently during puberty.

We've already talked about some changes *both* boys and girls go through, like getting taller, hair around the genitals, armpit hair, body odor, and acne. Now, let's look at changes specifi-

GIRL CHANGES: BECOMING A WOMAN

cally experienced by girls. These changes are very exciting, because they mean a girl is becoming a woman, and her body and mind are becoming mature.

Talking Points:

(As you talk, flip back to the female anatomy diagram on page 17 to use as a visual.)

Getting Bigger

- Do you remember how we talked about estrogen? (*See what your child remembers about this.*) Estrogen is the primary hormone that is responsible for changes in a girl's body during puberty. Estrogen plays a big role in all these changes.

- Both boys and girls get taller during puberty. Girls usually start getting taller before boys do, but boys quickly catch up. Around age 9, girls will often begin a growth spurt, but this can happen earlier or later.

- Both boys' and girls' bodies change their composition during puberty: this means both muscle and fat start growing in different areas more than before. But girls usually start to see more body fat in their upper arms, thighs, and upper back. A girls hips also often get wider. This isn't an unhealthy kind of fat, so it isn't anything a girl should worry about.

Hair Growth

- Look at your leg right now. Look really close. Do you see any hair on it right now? Even really small hairs? (*See if your child can see the small, fine hairs on their legs.*) Both boys and girls grow body hair in new places during puberty. The hair on their arms and legs will often grow darker and thicker than before. Some girls choose to start shaving their legs and their armpits around this time, depending on what the customs of her family is.

- The outer portion of a girl's private parts, the folds that are visible when she is not clothed is called the labia majora. During puberty, hair will begin to grow there. The hair growth can also extend to a girl's upper thighs as well.

GIRL CHANGES: BECOMING A WOMAN

Girl Talk: Moms, if you shave now would be a good time to show your daughter the razor you use. Talk about how often you shave and when. Explain to her how to use a razor safely. Make sure to answer any questions she has about this.

Breast Development

- For girls, puberty is the time when they begin developing larger breasts. It starts with what are called breast buds. These are firm, nickel-sized lumps girls can feel under their nipples. Sometimes both breast buds will form at the same time, but other times, one will start before the other one. This usually happens around 9 or 10, but for some girls it happens as early as 6 or 7, and others not until 13 or 14.

- These breast buds grow larger and rounder, as the breasts continue to grow throughout puberty. Breasts can vary in size greatly, and it has nothing to do with how soon or how late breast growth starts. Breast growth is just a sign that a girl's body is maturing. If the girl has a baby later on, she'll be able to breastfeed that baby with milk from her breasts. Her breasts will contain milk ducts and the hormone prolactin is produced after the birth of the baby which causes the breasts to begin making milk. Keep in mind, breast size doesn't have anything to do with the ability to breastfeed.

Girl Talk: Moms, now would be a good time to talk about any modesty standards you might have regarding undergarments.

GIRL CHANGES: BECOMING A WOMAN

Menstruation

- Part of what makes a baby are a woman's eggs. A girl's eggs are formed inside her ovaries. A woman has two ovaries inside her body.

- During puberty, usually a year and half to three years after breasts start to develop, girls start something called menstruation. The average age to start this is 12, but some girls start a couple years before this, while other girls start a couple years later.

- As a girl grows, one of the ovaries releases an egg typically around once a month. When an egg is released, it's called ovulation. If sperm from a man's body is there to fertilize this egg, the egg will be fertilized, and it will travel down something called the fallopian tube and attach itself to the wall of the uterus—also called the womb.

- The girl's body forms a layer of tissue and blood in the uterus to form a cushiony place for the egg in case a fertilized egg comes along.

- This fertilized egg, which is actually a very, very small developing baby, will grow in the uterus until it is time for the baby to be born.

Girl Talk: Moms, you may want to show your daughter different types of sanitary products that she may use when she begins her period. It's best to acquaint your daughter with these things before she starts her period, so she isn't completely caught off guard and knows what types of products she will be using. Talk about what they may feel during their period, such as cramping or feeling bloated, but also teach her that every woman experiences different things.

- Most of the time, there won't be sperm present to fertilize the egg, so the unfertilized egg will just travel down the fallopian tube and the body will get rid of it along with the extra blood and tissue in the uterus. All of this bloody material comes out of the vagina. The amount of blood a girl loses during a period varies from girl to girl. This time of bleeding is often called menses or a period.

GIRL CHANGES: BECOMING A WOMAN

...d typically lasts 3 to 7 days. It may seem kind of weird to think of bleeding for several days once a month, but it is actually a very healthy thing. It shows the girl her body is working properly and is maturing, and that she might become a mother some day.

- How often do you think this happens? (*See what your child thinks?*) The time between each period is called a girl's menstrual cycle. For some girls, the cycle is shorter, like 21 days. For most girls it's around 28 days. For some girls it's a little longer, like 45 days. It isn't uncommon for a girl's cycle to be irregular when it first begins—sometimes being shorter and sometimes being longer. Typically, it will settle into a more predictable cycle as she gets older. A girl will have a regular period—except when she is pregnant—for several decades.

- Girls often wear a special pad or cup to catch the blood, or they use a tampon to absorb the blood so it doesn't get on their clothing.

General Changes

- All of these changes are wonderful changes, because they are preparing a girl's body for becoming a wife and mother some day. Not everyone gets married when they grow up, but most people eventually do, and these physical changes make girls capable of eventually having sex and creating new life.

- It is important for girls to remember that God didn't make our sexual organs merely for our own pleasure, even though it is enjoyable for couples to have sex. God made our sexual organs so we could show love to the one we're married to. This is why God forbids people to have sex before they are married. We should never give ourselves physically to someone else unless we have committed ourselves to that person in marriage.

Girl Talk: You might find these changes a little strange at times, but remember I'm here to answer any questions you have. There are no dumb questions. No one expects you to understand these changes in your body. That's why I'm here to help you. If you want to know if something is normal, just ask!

GIRL CHANGES: BECOMING A WOMAN

Questions for Your Child:

1. Who is the one who made us male and female? *(God.)*

2. Let's see if you remember. What's it called when a girl bleeds a little from her vagina? *(Menstruation, menses, or a period.)*

3. When an egg is fertilized and is implanted on the wall of the uterus, does a girl have a period then? *(No.)*

4. Why did God make a woman to experience menstruation? *(So an egg could be released and possibly be fertilized by a man's sperm. This is what creates new life.)*

5. Of the changes in girls we just talked about, which one sounds the strangest to you? *(Allow your child to express his or her discomfort about any of the things mentioned in this lesson. Be sure to reassure him or her that these changes are all part of the body's transition to adulthood.)*

Prayer: God, thank You for creating the female body, built to be the perfect home for a new baby. Lord, help us to appreciate the changes that take place in puberty, because they are Your ways of changing us from children into adults. Amen.

BOY CHANGES: BECOMING A MAN

Opening Thought:

What do you remember about what we talked about last time—the way girls change as they go through puberty? (*See how much your child remembers.*) We talked about girls last time, so what should be talk about now? (*Boys.*)

Most boys begin puberty sometime between 9 and 14 years old, but there isn't any way of knowing for sure when your body will decide it's time to start. Puberty typically lasts anywhere from 2 to 5 years. Everyone's a little different, but what happens during puberty is pretty much the same for all boys.

Scripture Reading: Genesis 1:26-27 (again)

Explanation: We read this same scripture last time. Do you remember, what we said about this passage? (*God created both male and female. Men and women are similar in many ways.*)

These verses of the Bible say that humankind—both male and female—are created in the image of God. What do you think this means? (*Men and women both deserve the same respect.*)

While there are numerous similarities between men and women, you probably can tell by just looking at the outside of people that we're also very different. When it comes to the sex organs of men and women—they have a very different way they function and different purposes as well.

We talked about some of the changes both boys and girls go through. We talked about changes that girls go through. We talked about how their bodies, during puberty, go through changes that make them capable of growing babies.

Today, we'll talk more about how God has designed boys to grow and develop into men.

BOY CHANGES: BECOMING A MAN

Talking Points:

(As you talk, flip back to the male anatomy diagram on page 17 to use as a visual.)

Getting Bigger

- Do you remember how we talked about testosterone? (*See what your child remembers about this.*) Testosterone is the primary hormone that is responsible for changes in a boy's body during puberty. Testosterone plays a big role in all these changes.

- Both boys and girls get taller during puberty. While girls usually start getting taller before boys do, boys catch up and often end up being taller, on average, than most girls. When puberty is in full swing, boys can grow around 4 inches a year!

- Both boys and girls experience muscle growth during puberty, but boys experience it much more than girls do. Over time, their muscles get stronger in their legs, arms, chest, shoulders—all over their bodies. It is important as boys grow for them to eat nutritious whole foods (not processed junk food!) and get physical exercise.

- Some boys will feel a tenderness under their nipples during puberty. This is normal and isn't something to be concerned about. It's just a boy's body getting used to all the new hormones. It is temporary—eventually going away in adulthood.

Hair Growth

- Both boys and girls grow body hair in new places, but boys also grow hair on their face and on their chest. Some time during puberty, a lot of boys learn how to shave their faces, depending on the customs of their family. What are the different ways you see men wear their facial hair? (*Full beard, just a mustache, longer sideburns, etc.*)

Boy Talk: Dads, you may want to show your son the razor you use to shave your face. Talk to him about how often you shave and when.

Voice Changes

- Both boys' and girls' voices change during puberty, but boys' voices usually change the most. In fact, as these changes are going on, boys might notice their voice will squeak and crack for a few months. Everyone has a larynx, also called a voice box. For boys, this tube shaped organ gets much longer and thicker, which makes their voice a lot deeper. Do you know anyone with a really deep voice? (*See if your child names a friend or relative with a low, bass voice.*)

- As the larynx grows, the protective material around it also grows and comes together at an angle, so as a boy grows he can see part of his larynx sticking out. People often call this an "Adam's Apple," but it isn't actually an apple.

Penis, Testicles, and Ejaculation

- What's the organ called that hangs down in front of a boy's body? (*A penis.*) Did you know that during puberty the penis thickens and lengthens over a period of several years?

- Boys also have two testicles. These hang down underneath the penis in sack of skin and muscle called the scrotum. During puberty, a boy's testicles will grow considerably.

- There are a couple functions the penis has. Can you guess what one of them is?

- First, when a man's bladder fills with urine, the body eventually wants to get rid of it. The urine can travel through something called the urethra which is a duct inside the penis. So, the penis is the organ men use to urinate. This is nothing new for a boy—both boys and girls urinate before they're even born.

- The second important thing the penis does has to do with what's inside the testicles. Testicles hold very special cells that are important because they are what helps make a baby. Do you know what they are called? (*Sperm.*)

- When a sperm fertilizes a woman's egg inside her body, a baby is made, and the penis is designed by God to get sperm inside a woman's body.

- A man's penis is full of blood vessels. When these blood vessels fill with blood, this makes his penis very hard and straight. This is called an erection.

- Now, from the time they are babies, boys get erections, so this is nothing new. But after puberty starts, a boy's body starts making a fluid called semen. Semen is a mixture of sugars, vitamins, and other chemicals that sperm love to swim in.

BOY CHANGES: BECOMING A MAN

- During puberty, after semen is created, a boy's body is capable of what's called ejaculation, which just means "to eject a fluid." When a boy gets sexually excited, he will often get an erection, and eventually muscles near the penis will push semen through the urethra and out of the body. Inside this semen there are about 180,000 sperm cells, though there can be a whole lot more.

- The reason why boys can get erections and the reason why they ejaculate is because of how God designed husbands and wives to have sex. When a man's penis is stiff and straight, it can more easily go inside a woman's vagina. When he ejaculates, this sends the sperm into her body so they can swim their way to the egg, possibly making a baby.

- Boys find they might have more erections during puberty, and this is normal. Boys might also have something called nocturnal emissions—sometimes called a wet dream—when his body will ejaculate while he is sleeping. This is just one of the body's normal ways of getting rid of extra semen.

Boy Talk: Having a nocturnal emission doesn't hurt, but there is a possibility you might wake up in the middle of one. Some boys might be embarrassed about nocturnal emissions, but you can't control them or stop them from happening, so they are nothing to be ashamed of. *(Now might be a good time to talk to your boys about what they should do to clean up if they wake up in the middle of the night or in the morning after having a nocturnal emission.)*

General Changes

- All of these changes are wonderful changes, because they are preparing a boy's body for becoming a husband and father some day. Not everyone gets married when they grow up, but most people eventually do, and these physical changes make boys capable of eventually having sex and creating new life.

- It is also really important for boys to remember that God didn't make our sexual organs merely for our own pleasure, even though it is enjoyable to have sex. God made our sexual organs so we could show love to the one we're married to. From what you remember in the Bible, does God want us to have sex before we are married? (*No.*) Why not? (*Because sex is an intimate act that binds us to another person, and because having sex means being open to creating new life. If we have sex with someone we are not married to, we bond emotionally and physically with that person, and if we are not committed to that person, this sets us up for a lot of hurt. It also means we could conceive a child, and this means a lot of children grow up in homes where they don't have a mom and a dad to raise them.*)

Boy Talk: You might find these changes a little strange at times, but remember I'm here to answer any questions you have. There are no dumb questions. No one expects you to understand these changes in your body. That's why I'm here to help you. If you want to know if something is normal, just ask!

Questions for Your Child:

1. Who is the one who made us male and female? *(God.)*

2. Let's see if you remember. What's it called when a boy's penis is very hard and straight? *(An erection.)*

3. What's it called when semen comes out of the boy's penis? *(Ejaculation.)*

4. Why did God make a man able to get an erection and ejaculate? *(So he could have sex with a woman and release sperm into her. This is so they can conceive a baby.)*

5. Which of the changes in boys we just talked about sounds the strangest to you? *(Allow your child to express his or her discomfort about any of the things mentioned in this lesson. Be sure to reassure him or her that these changes are all part of the body's transition to adulthood.)*

Prayer: God, thank You for creating the male body. Lord, help us to appreciate the changes that take place in puberty, because they are Your ways of changing us from children into adults. In Jesus' name, Amen.

CHANGES IN DESIRE: THE GOODNESS OF SEXUAL ATTRACTION

Opening Thought:

Have I ever told you about the first time I went on a date with (*name of spouse or first person you ever dated*)? (*Tell your child the story of that experience. Be sure to emphasize the feelings you had about the way the other person looked: the way they were dressed, the way they smiled or laughed, the things you really enjoyed about their company.*)

This is another big part of puberty: physical attraction. Let's read a short passage from the Bible about that.

Scripture Reading: Song of Solomon 1:15-17

Explanation: In this poem, there are two speakers who are on a date outside. The first is the man, King Solomon, who is looking at the woman saying, "You are beautiful." He likens her eyes to doves because they look gentle, innocent, and loving. She speaks back to him and tells him he is very handsome. Using her imagination, she says the grass they are on is like a green bed and the surrounding trees are like the tall, wooden beams of their house. She is daydreaming, thinking, "I think I'm in love with this man. Whenever we are together, I feel at home."

All throughout the Bible, there are stories of men and women being physically attracted to one another, and this is another really important part of puberty. Actually, boys and girls tend to feel their first hint of physical attraction to others around the age of 10, even if only a little bit. Have you ever seen someone of the opposite sex and found yourself thinking about how cute they are, or have you ever seen someone really attractive and caught yourself staring at that person? (*Allow your child to open up about specific times when this might have happened.*)

CHANGES IN DESIRE: THE GOODNESS OF SEXUAL ATTRACTION

Talking Points:

- When you think someone is attractive, you may find yourself wanting to be around them more or watch them more. You might feel this way about a friend—even a close friend you've grown up with—or just someone you see from time to time. You might feel this way about someone you see on TV or in a movie. You might even feel this way about an older person you know. Something about the way their face looks or the way their body looks just draws your eyes, or something about they way they talk or smile really attracts you. People sometimes call this getting a crush on someone.

- There are two important things to remember about physical attraction. First, you must remember that it is good, so we should thank God for it. Second is that it can be very powerful, so we should not let it control us. Let's think about both of these things.

- First, physical attraction is good because God made it. As you grow into an adult, your brain is wired to find the opposite sex very compelling. The sense of physical attraction is a gift from God because we are physical creatures. Just as God made certain foods to taste good, He made certain things in nature to look good. He made the opposite sex to look attractive to us. This way, as we get older and into a romantic relationship with someone, we can be attracted to that person inside and out—we enjoy their personality, their character, and the way they look. (*Parents, take a moment to talk about when you first met your spouse or when you first found yourself physically attracted to your spouse. Talk about one or two things that stood out to you physically.*)

- But second, physical attraction is also very powerful. There are times we can get a crush on someone and it feels like they are all we think about. We might find ourselves daydreaming about them or staring at them when they are around us. If we keep thinking about them, we might start daydreaming about what it would be like to hold their hand or kiss them, or what it would be like if they were in love with us.

- Physical attraction is so powerful, if we aren't careful it can turn into lust. Lust is the word used in the Bible for when we strongly crave someone else in a sexual way. God only wants married people to strongly desire one another that way because in marriage we can act on those desires and show physical, sexual love to our spouse.

- Lust is also powerful the other way around, feeling like you're obsessed with being attractive to others. You might start to think a lot about the clothing you wear, the look of your body or your face, or if others are paying attention to you. Of course, it is important to take care of the bodies God gave to us, but we don't want to ever get obsessed with our body image. God made our bodies, and God doesn't make junk. Besides, comparing how we look to how others look makes us really miserable, because our culture has a very narrow definition of beauty. Instead, God wants us to focus on our character—the way we love Him and love others—because this the kind of beauty that really matters.

- In the Bible we read a lot of stories about how people misused sex. Some people feel so overwhelmed with desire, they even abuse others in a sexual way. Please, keep this in mind: as you grow up, not only is it important to guard your heart against lust, remember there might be times when others lust after you. If others try to touch the private parts of your body without your permission, it is important you tell me about it so we try to make sure it doesn't happen again. Can you think of a time in your life when someone might have ever touched your private parts in a way that made you feel uncomfortable? (*Allow your child to talk to you about any experiences he or she might have had.*)

- So keep these two things in mind. It isn't wrong to feel attracted to someone. It's a good thing. God likes it when we appreciate the way His creation looks, and that includes other people. But we should also remember physical attraction is powerful, and if we aren't careful, we might find ourselves being controlled by our desires and lusting after someone else or desiring to be lusted after.

- As you get older, you'll notice this physical attraction more and more, and as you do just remember to thank God for it and to ask God to help you to control it so it doesn't control you.

- One last important thing to say about all these talks we've had, while this is all very interesting, it is important that *parents* share this with their children. Your friends have parents who will explain to them how their body will be changing and what that means. Don't bring this up around them, and if anyone brings it up to you, just tell them it isn't an appropriate conversation.

Questions for Your Child:

1. Because physical attraction is so powerful, sometimes people think it is bad thing. They are afraid of its power, so they just try to convince themselves it's evil. Why is this wrong? *(Because God made it. God created it as a good thing and we should never treat it like it's evil.)*

2. Because physical attraction is good and enjoyable, sometimes people think lust is no big deal. They enjoy it so much, they don't care if they lust after others. Why is this wrong? *(Because God wants us to save those strong feelings of desire for marriage. When we strongly crave someone sexually and we aren't married to them, our desire will either frustrate us, or it will move us to try to get close to them in a sexual way.)*

3. Why do you think God made physical attraction so powerful? *(Because if we get married some day, he wants us to really enjoy our spouse.)*

Prayer: God, thank You for creating physical attraction. Just one glance from someone's eye can captivate us (Song of Solomon 4:9). Help us to remember, however, that physical beauty doesn't last (Proverbs 31:30), that the kind of beauty that lasts forever is a gentle and quiet spirit (1 Peter 3:4). Help us to appreciate this gift of physical attraction, but to never look only at outward appearance. We often are too focused the way someone looks, but You look at the heart (1 Samuel 16:7). Amen.

CHANGES

WHAT'S NEXT?

This book is designed to serve more as a bridge—the middle book in a trilogy. Our first book, _The Talk_, was about giving children in the middle childhood years a basic understanding of biblical sexuality, introducing elementary concepts like what it means to be male or female, how babies are made, and the importance of marriage.

This book is more about how to think rightly about one's body during puberty, anticipating the changes that girls and boys go through as they mature into adults capable of sexual reproduction.

Our next book (coming out in the Spring of 2016) will be about how to steward one's sexuality during puberty. It will cover concepts such as respecting the opposite sex, guarding your heart, modesty, lust, masturbation, homosexuality, and biblical masculinity and femininity. As your child grows and matures, these will be topics your child is naturally curious about, especially as they begin to show a physical or emotional attraction to others.

Gospel-Centered Optimism

In Western culture, we tend to have a pessimistic view of teens: teenagers are nothing more than a collection of rampant, unruly hormones. This is a subtle but nonetheless bold denial that the gospel applies to teens. After all, hormones don't repent and believe in anything.

Of course, sin is very much alive in the hearts of teenagers—even in teens who have a genuine faith in Christ. But as Christian parents we need to approach our teens with a _gospel-centered optimism_, a strong belief that the gospel applies to and can transform anyone, even hormonally-challenged people.

Notice, we're not advocating some kind of a carte blanche, generic optimism, as if we believe our teens are "good kids" deep down (without Christ). Nor are we pushing for a law-centered optimism, as if all our teens need is more boundaries, more rules, and more restrictions in order to get in line. Nor are we advocating sin-centered pessimism, as if our kids are just lost causes. None of these approaches is biblical.

WHAT'S NEXT?

As the teen years approach, the most important things we can offer our kids is *hope* and *humility*: hope that the gospel can reach them right where they are, and humility to admit that we are more like our kids than we often care to admit—we too desperately need Jesus to rescue us from our sins.

Be the Adult You Want Your Child to Become

The emotions associated with puberty vary greatly from child to child, but one of the most important things you can do as a parent is to not allow your own emotions to get the best of you.

You must strive to model the kind of adult reactions you want your son or daughter to have. We want to be able to say to our children as Paul did to his disciples, "Be imitators of me, as I am of Christ" (1 Corinthians 11:1).

Freedom with Boundaries

Teens need both the freedom to explore and clear guardrails to direct their course. Often the wisdom of good parenting is learning the balance between adult-like freedoms and childlike boundaries.

The Internet – The World Wide Web is a microcosm of the world—anything and everything possible to see contained in the palm of your hand. It's like the big city: there are some streets you want your son or daughter to explore, and there are others you would prefer they stay away from.

While Internet filters can be helpful, we need to remember teens are budding adults and they won't always live in a world with fences or filters. The teen years are an ideal time to train them for that world, and one of the best tools to do this is Internet accountability software, like Covenant Eyes. It gives your children the freedom to explore online without blockades, but they will do so knowing you get a report every week of all the websites they visited and all the questionable searches they made. Just knowing Mom or Dad will know often keeps temptations at bay, and when something questionable does pop up, you'll know about it and can talk about it in an informed way.

Media Choices – More than just being restricted from certain kinds of media, teens need to develop a sense of "media discernment." This means an ability to analyze the messages of television shows, movies, video games, and music. This can only come with practice and is best done with you, the parent.

Take time to enjoy media with your child and look for the subtle messages embedded in media—especially messages about love, sex, relationships, family, and God. Rather than merely "laying down the law" about what media should and should not be consumed, default to dialogue with your teens about why the messages of certain kinds of media are not healthy or godly.

Opposite Sex – Every family has their own dating and courtship norms, even if they aren't stated very clearly. As parents, make your expectations about opposite-sex interactions very clear, and be prepared to give a basic biblical rationale behind those expectations.

What social norms will both encourage your teen to interact with and get to know those of the opposite sex, to get to know the kind of person they "click with"? What norms will help your teen to guard his or her heart from needless attachment too early? What are some basic rules for interaction (curfews, appropriate and inappropriate touch, etc.)?

A Promise to Remember

As our children grow into adults, we all want them to steward their sexuality well. God tells us we can be delivered from sexual temptations as we rely on His wisdom (Proverbs 2:16), and God has chosen parents to deliver that wisdom to our children.

> My son, if you receive my words
> and treasure up my commandments with you,
> making your ear attentive to wisdom
> and inclining your heart to understanding;
> yes, if you call out for insight
> and raise your voice for understanding,
> if you seek it like silver
> and search for it as for hidden treasures,
> then you will understand the fear of the Lord
> and find the knowledge of God. (Proverbs 2:1-5)

IMAGINE...

getting a report in your e-mail inbox of the websites your kids visit, the search terms they use, and the YouTube videos they watch.

IMAGINE...

protecting them online with a filter that's tailored to their needs and grows with them as they mature.

IMAGINE...

that protection following you and your family on all the computers, smartphones, and tablets you use.

IMAGINE...

an online accountability program that guards the hearts of parents as well as kids.

CovenantEyes.com

Get a Family Account with

Covenant Eyes
Internet Accountability and Filtering

Get a unique username for every person in your family (unlimited usernames), on as many devices as you need.

Stop imagining, and see how much safer your family can be online.

Try it out now. Use the promo code

TheTalk

and get your first month of service FREE!

Made in the USA
Columbia, SC
24 February 2022